Miracle of Love

Adult Coloring book

By

S.B. Nozaz

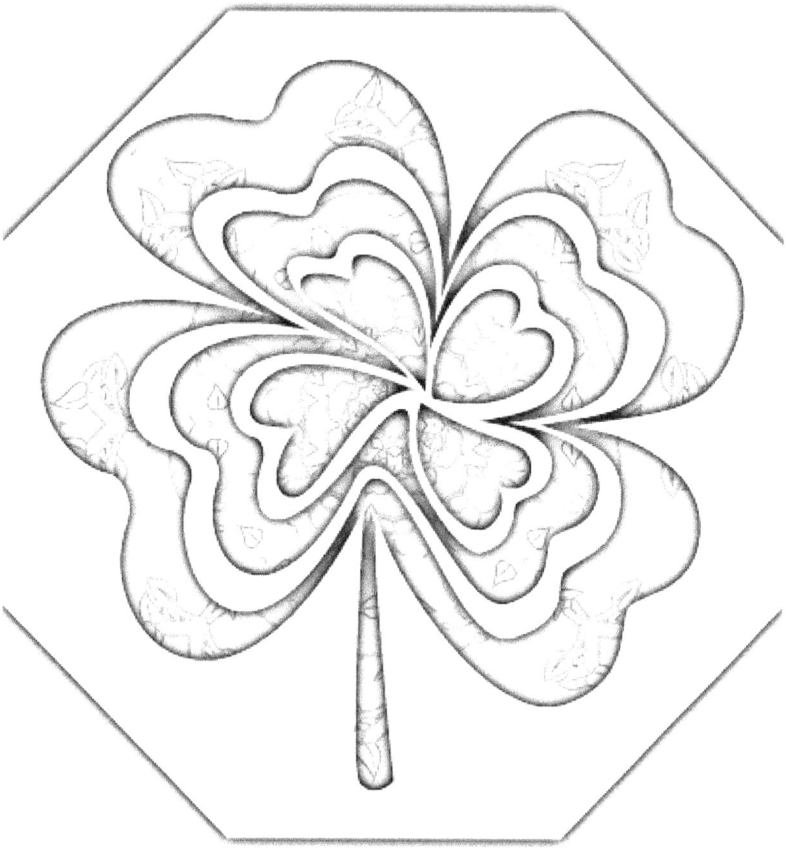

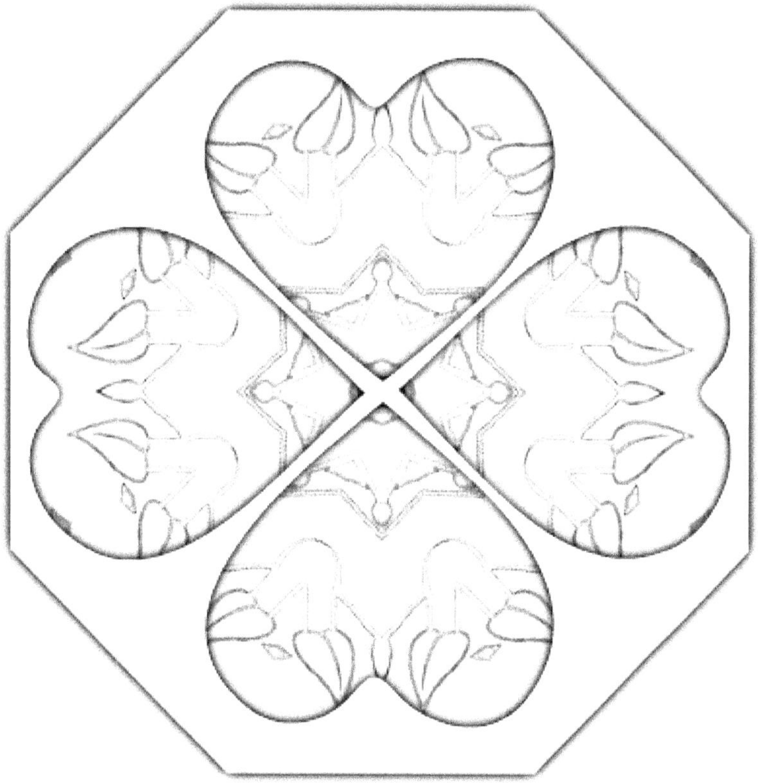

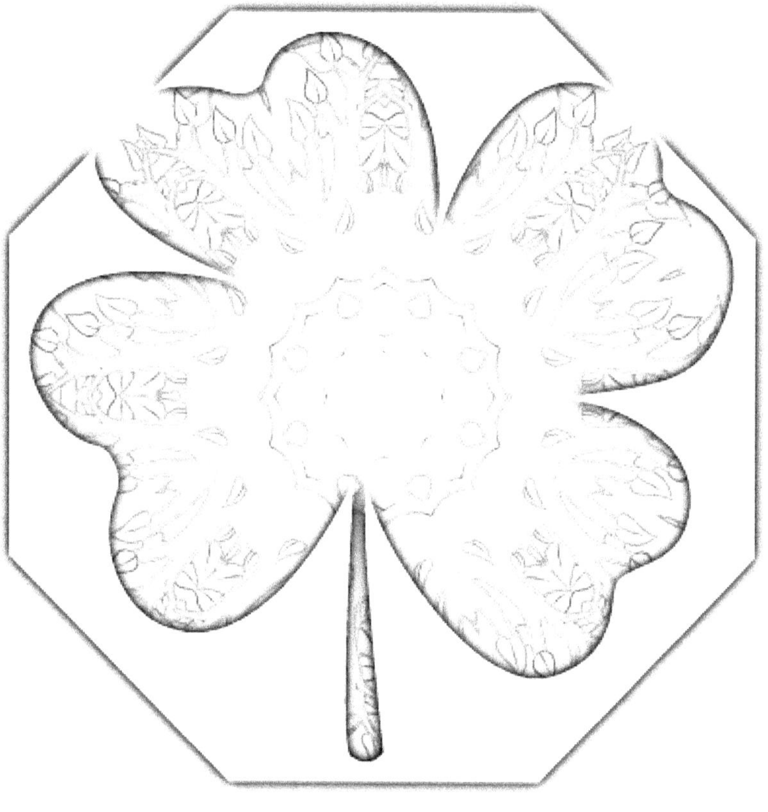

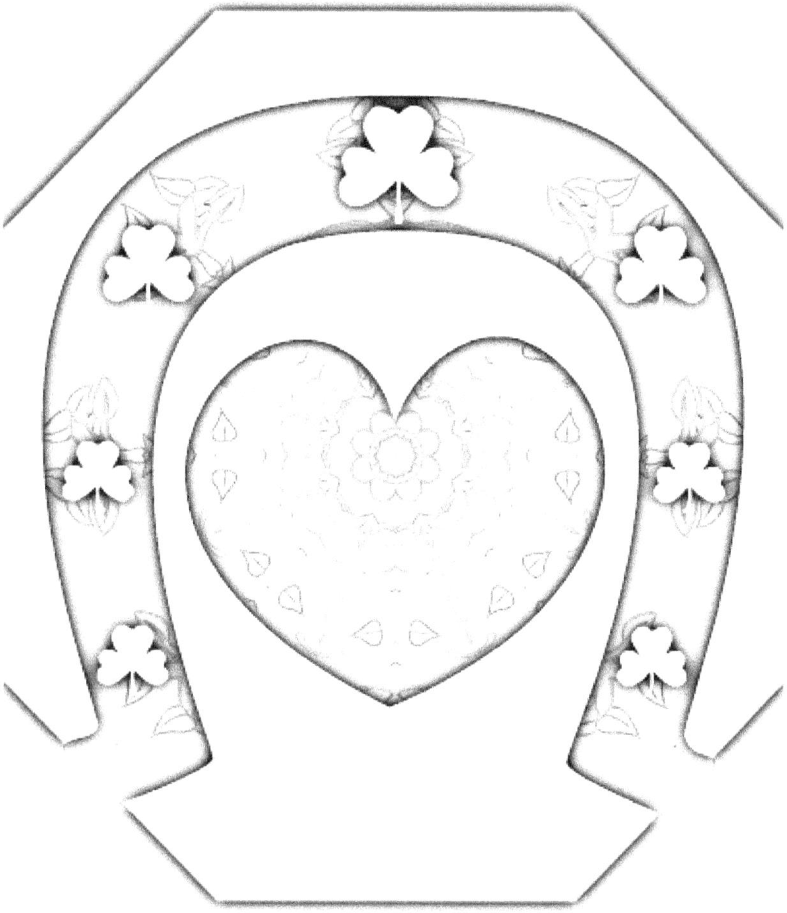

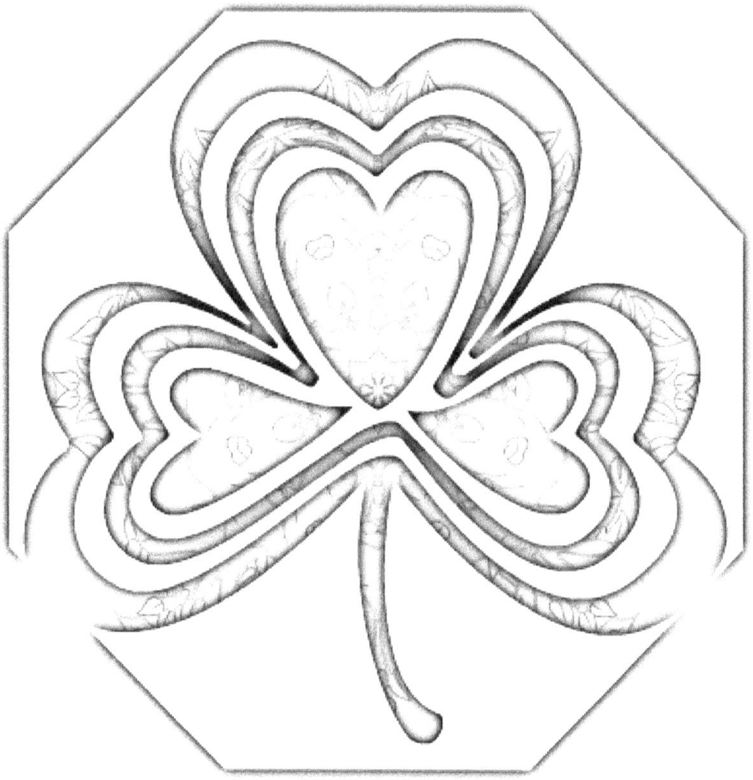

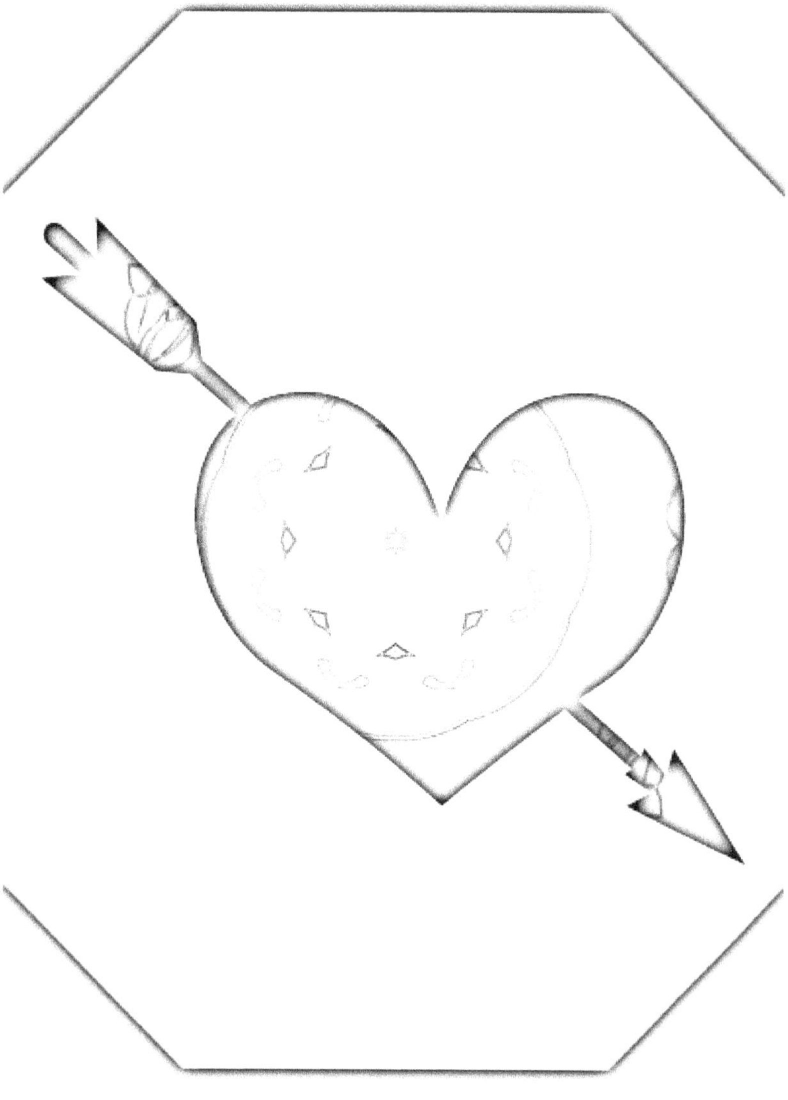

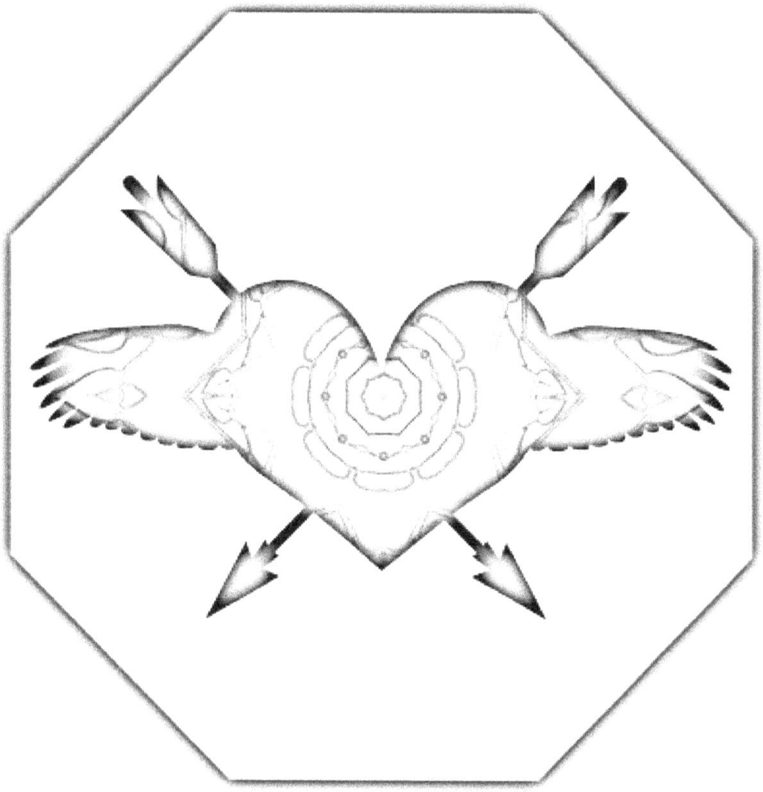

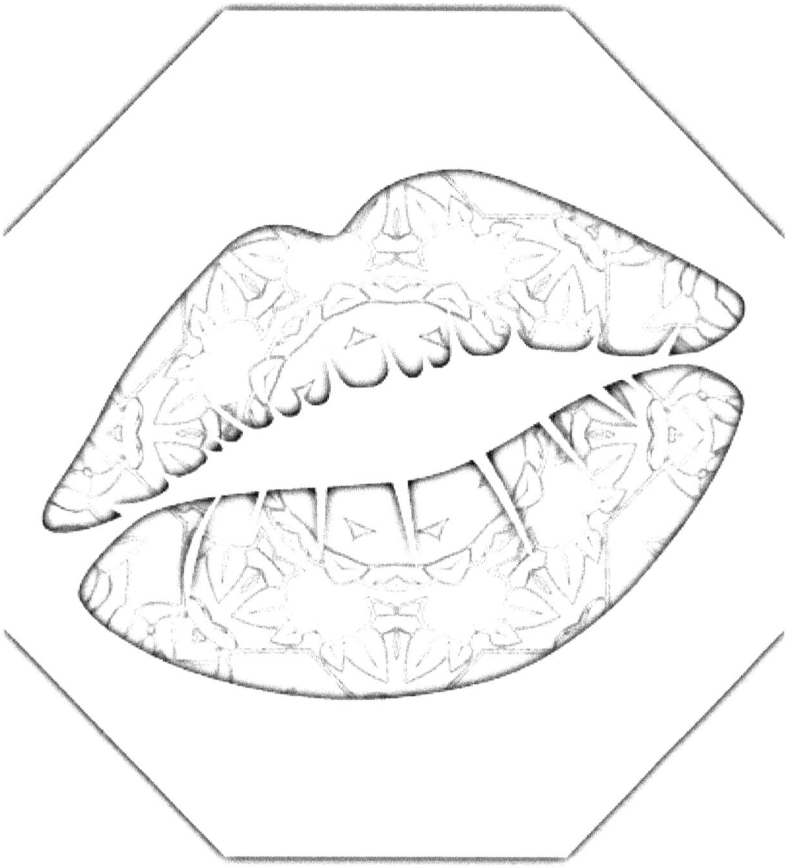

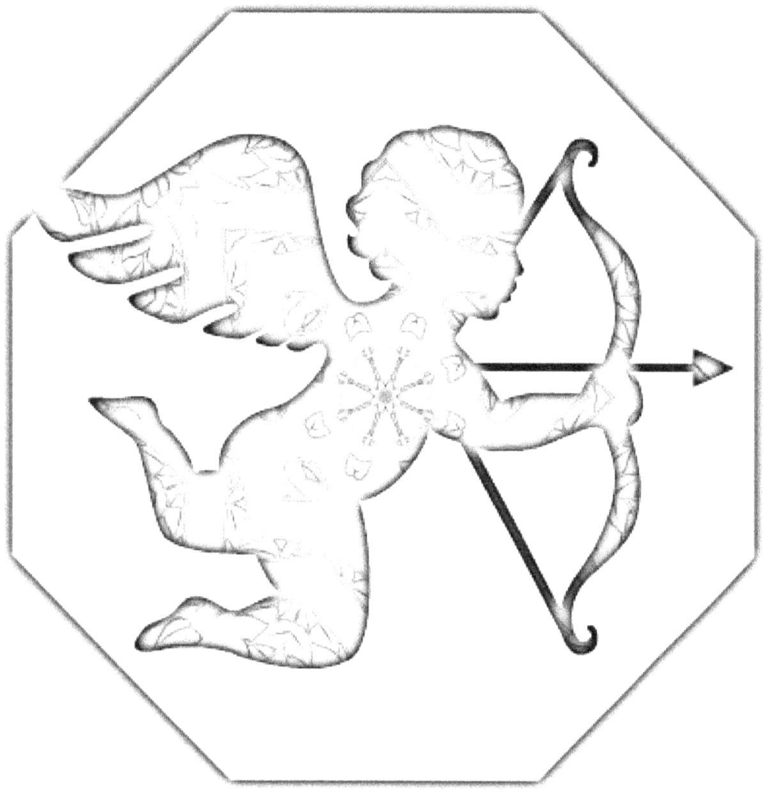

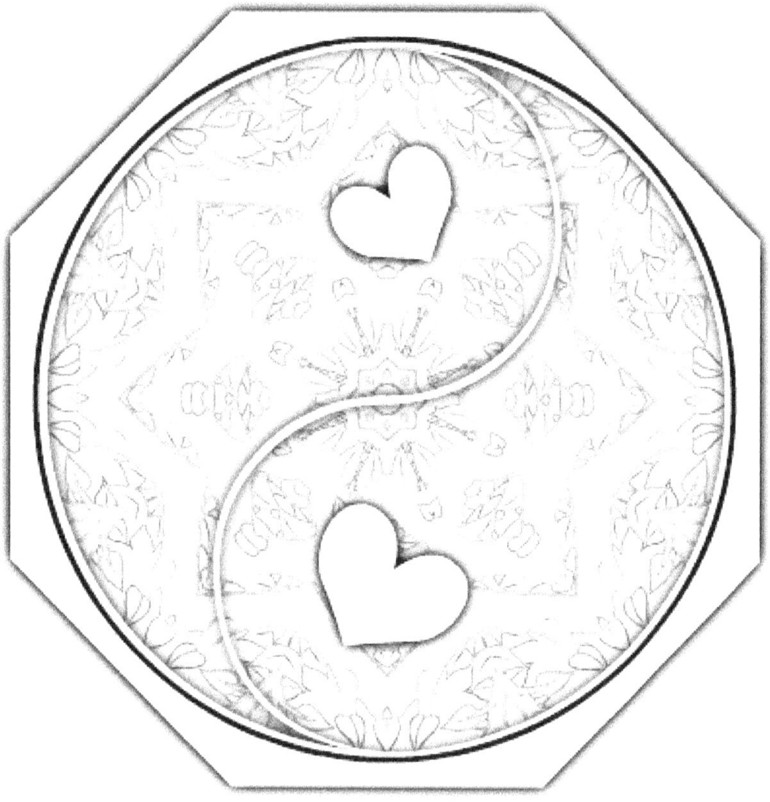

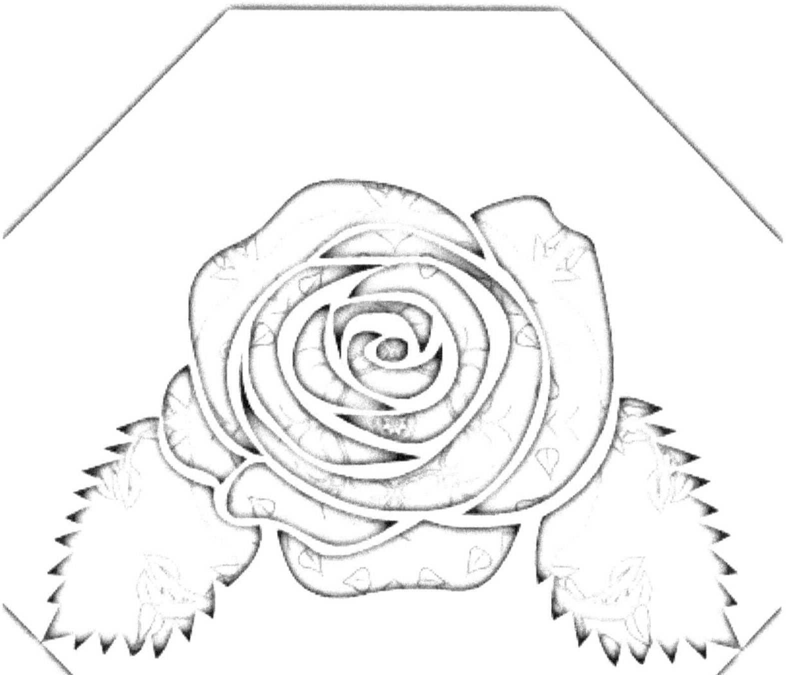

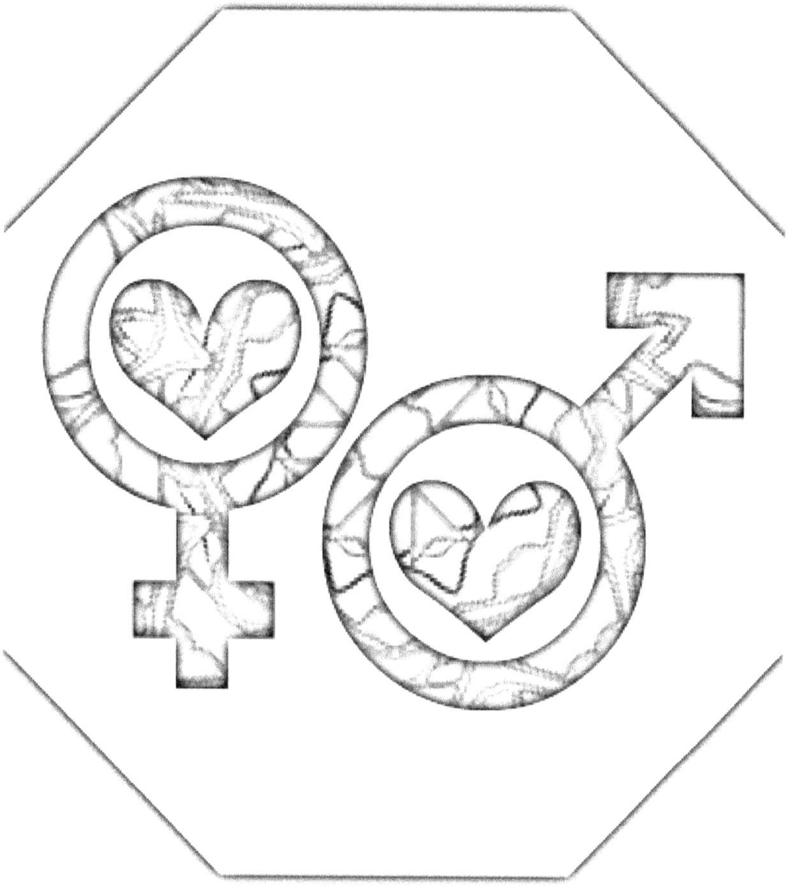

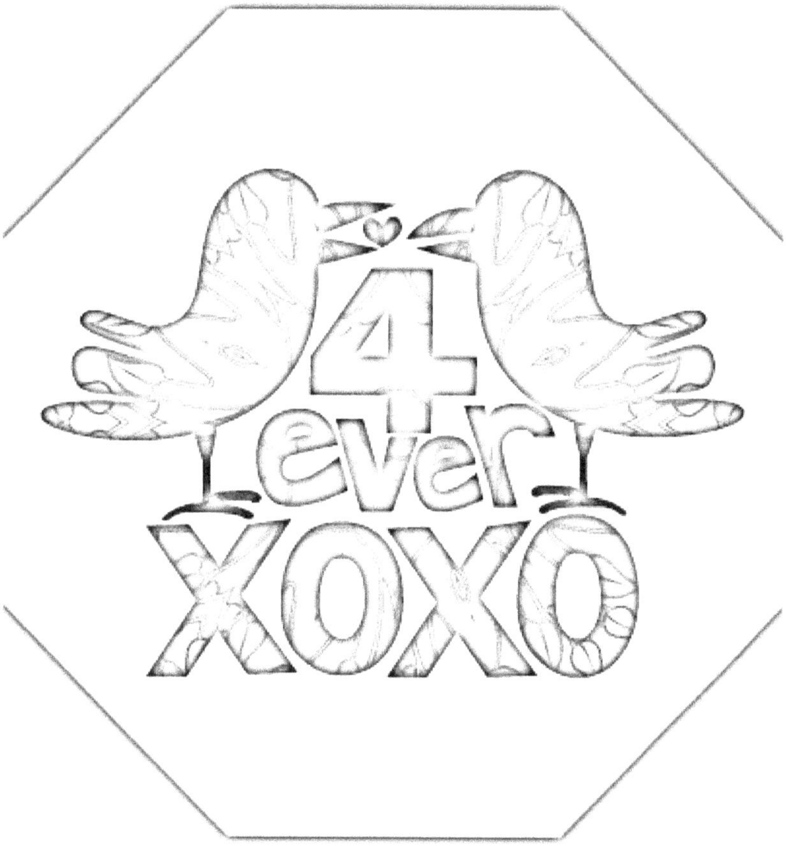
4
ever
XOXO

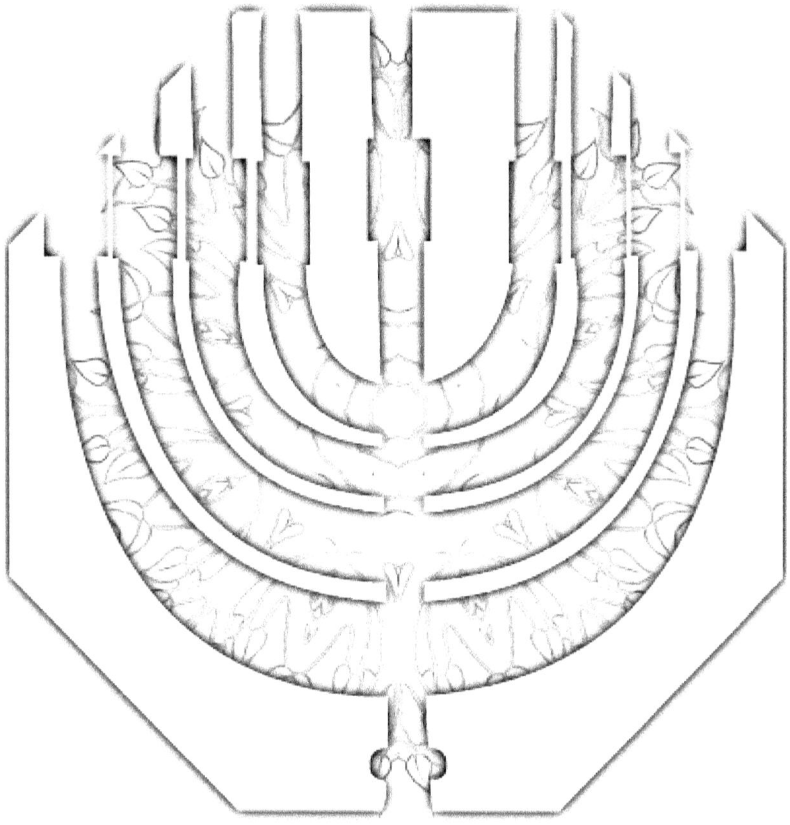

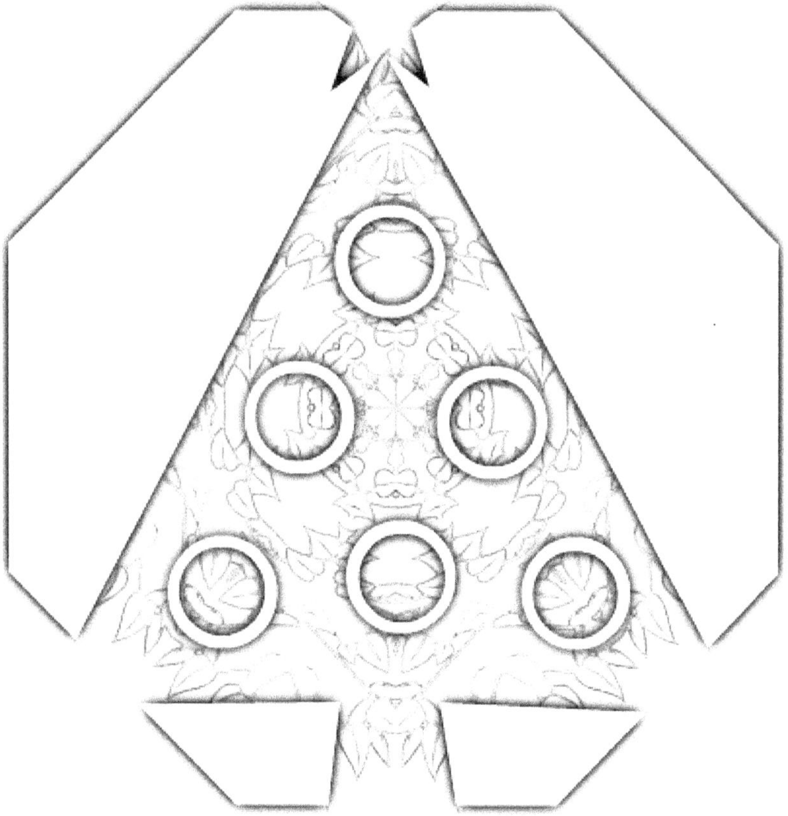

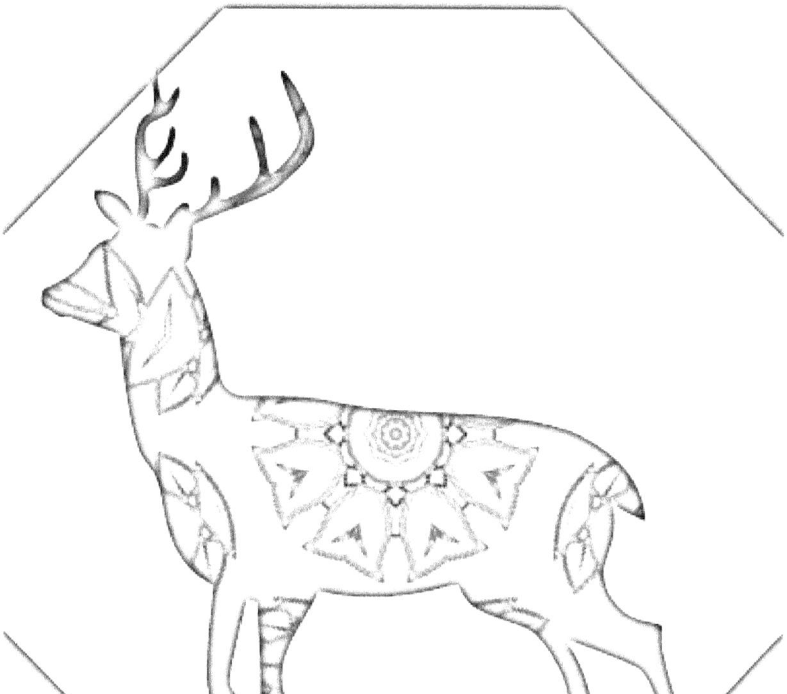

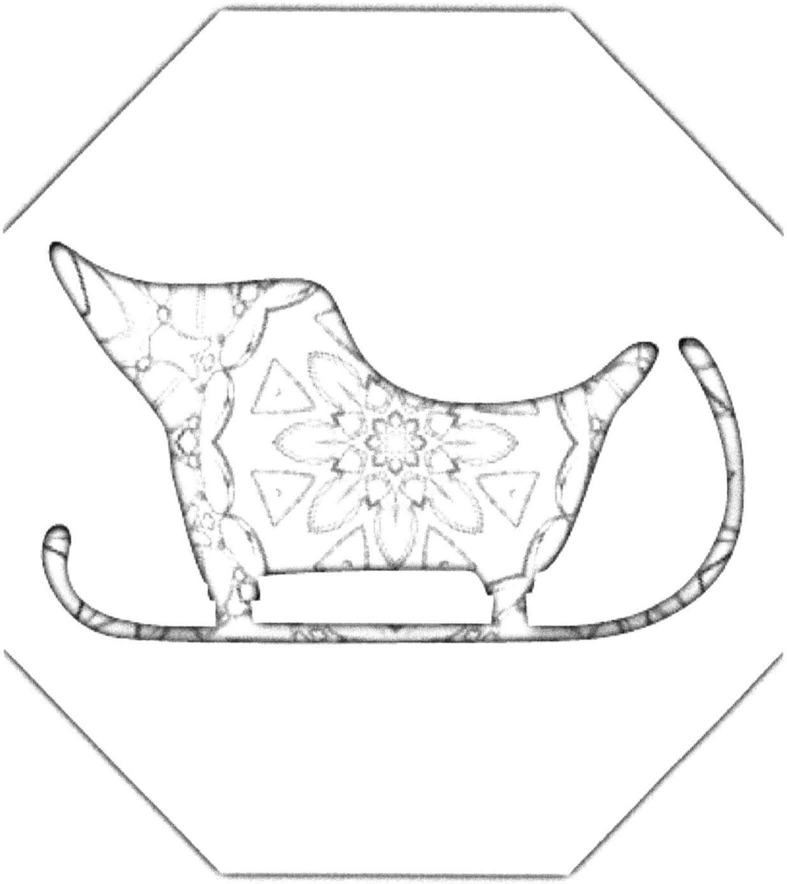

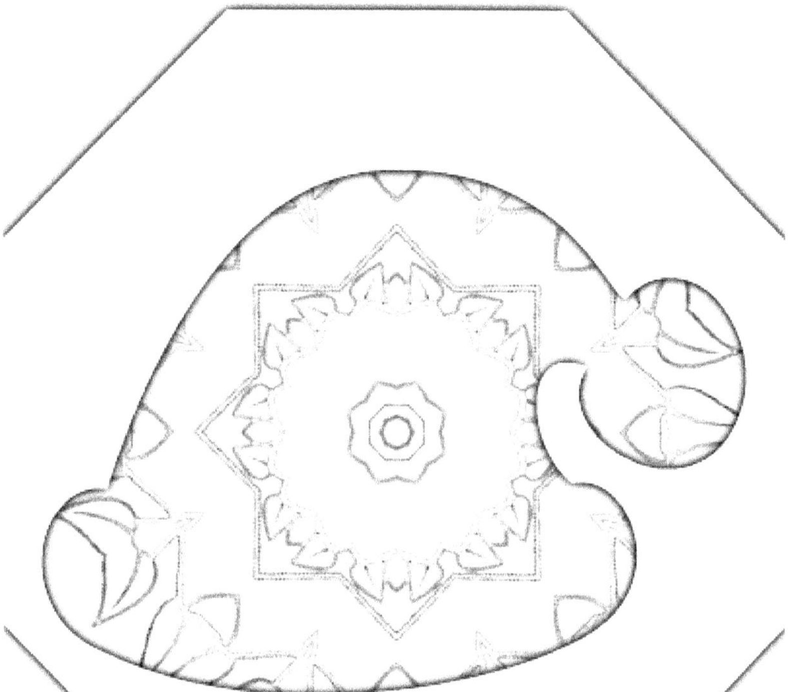

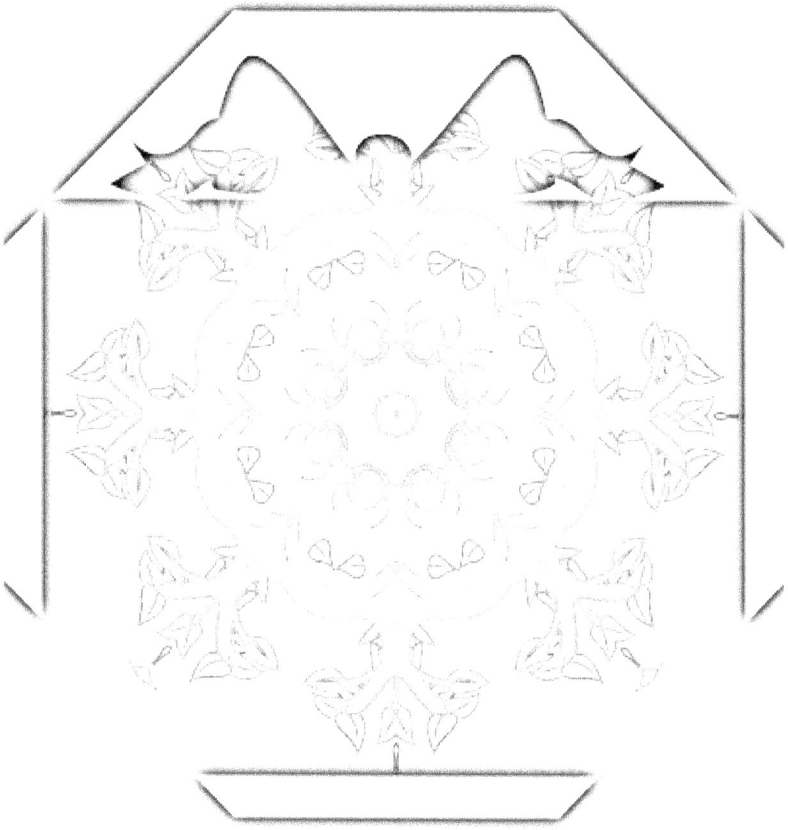

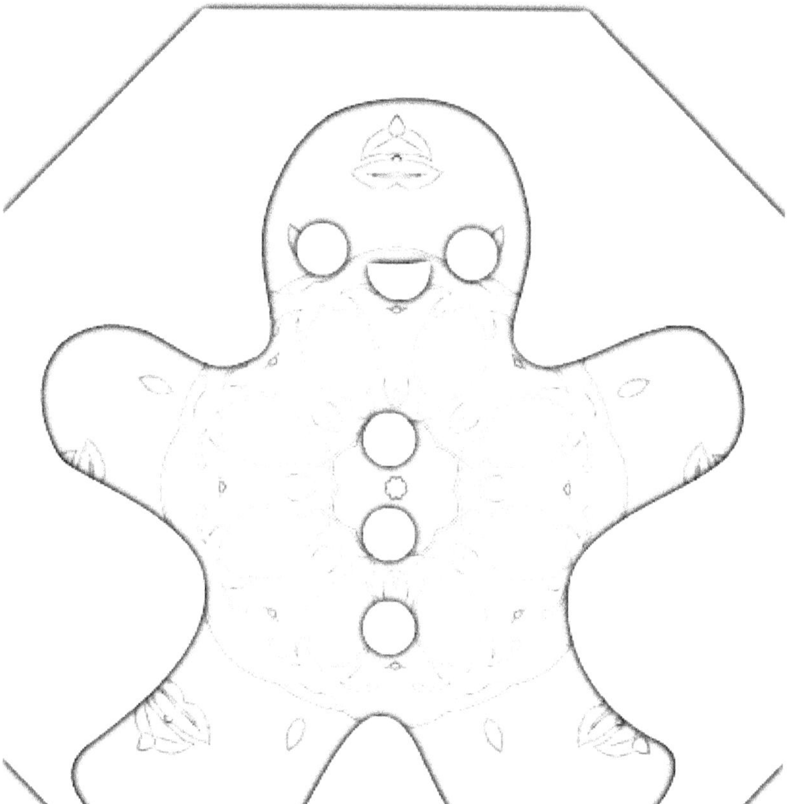

Note

www.ingramcontent.com/pod-product-compliance
Lightning Source LLC
Chambersburg PA
CBHW080651180526
45168CB00008B/3382
9781517597542